**PROTOCOL
AMENDING THE CONVENTION BETWEEN
THE UNITED STATES OF AMERICA AND CANADA
WITH RESPECT TO TAXES ON INCOME AND ON CAPITAL
DONE AT WASHINGTON ON 26 SEPTEMBER 1980
AS AMENDED BY THE PROTOCOLS DONE ON 14 JUNE 1983,
28 MARCH 1984, 17 MARCH 1995 AND 29 JULY 1997**

The United States of America and Canada, hereinafter referred to as the "Contracting States",

DESIRING to conclude a Protocol amending the Convention between the United States of

America and Canada with Respect to Taxes on Income and on Capital done at Washington on

26 September 1980, as amended by the Protocols done on 14 June 1983, 28 March 1984, 17

March 1995 and 29 July 1997 (hereinafter referred to as the "Convention"),

HAVE AGREED as follows:

Article 1

Paragraph 1 of Article III (General Definitions) of the Convention shall be amended by deleting the word "and" at the end of subparagraph (i), by replacing the period at the end of subparagraph (j) with "; and", and by adding the following subparagraph:

(k)   The term "national" of a Contracting State means:

(i)   Any individual possessing the citizenship or nationality of that State; and

(ii)   Any legal person, partnership or association deriving its status as such from the laws in force in that State.

Article 2

1.   Paragraph 3 of Article IV (Residence) of the Convention shall be deleted and replaced by the following:

3.   Where by reason of the provisions of paragraph 1, a company is a resident of both Contracting States, then

(a)   If it is created under the laws in force in a Contracting State, but not under the laws in force in the other Contracting State, it shall be deemed to be a resident only of the first-mentioned State; and

(b)   In any other case, the competent authorities of the Contracting States shall endeavor to settle the question of residency by mutual agreement and determine the mode of application of this Convention to the company. In the absence of such agreement, the company shall not be considered a resident of either Contracting State for purposes of claiming any benefits under this Convention.

2.   Article IV (Residence) of the Convention shall be amended by adding the following after paragraph 5:

6.   An amount of income, profit or gain shall be considered to be derived by a person who is a resident of a Contracting State where:

> (a)   The person is considered under the taxation law of that State to have derived the amount through an entity (other than an entity that is a resident of the other Contracting State); and
>
> (b)   By reason of the entity being treated as fiscally transparent under the laws of the first-mentioned State, the treatment of the amount under the taxation law of that State is the same as its treatment would be if that amount had been derived directly by that person.

7.   An amount of income, profit or gain shall be considered not to be paid to or derived by a person who is a resident of a Contracting State where:

> (a)   The person is considered under the taxation law of the other Contracting State to have derived the amount through an entity that is not a resident of the first-mentioned State, but by reason of the entity not being treated as fiscally transparent under the laws of that State, the treatment of the amount under the taxation law of that State is not the same as its treatment would be if that amount had been derived directly by that person; or
>
> (b)   The person is considered under the taxation law of the other Contracting State to have received the amount from an entity that is a resident of that other State, but by reason of the entity being treated as fiscally transparent under the laws of the first-mentioned State, the treatment of the amount under the taxation law of that State is not the same as its treatment would be if that entity were not treated as fiscally transparent under the laws of that State.

Article 3

1.   The first sentence of paragraph 6 of Article V (Permanent Establishment) of the Convention shall be amended by deleting the word "and" preceding the first reference to paragraph 5, inserting a comma, and adding the words "and 9," following that reference to paragraph 5.

2.   Paragraph 9 of Article V (Permanent Establishment) of the Convention shall be deleted and replaced by the following two paragraphs:

> 9.   Subject to paragraph 3, where an enterprise of a Contracting State provides services in the other Contracting State, if that enterprise is found not to have a permanent establishment in that other State by virtue of the preceding paragraphs of this Article, that enterprise shall be deemed to provide those services through a permanent establishment in that other State if and only if:
>
> > (a)   Those services are performed in that other State by an individual who is present in that other State for a period or periods aggregating 183 days or more in any twelve-month period, and, during that period or periods, more than 50 percent of the gross active business revenues of the enterprise consists of income derived from the services performed in that other State by that individual; or
> >
> > (b)   The services are provided in that other State for an aggregate of 183 days or more in any twelve-month period with respect to the same or connected project for customers who are either residents of that other State or who maintain a permanent establishment in that other State and the services are provided in respect of that permanent establishment.
>
> 10.   For the purposes of this Convention, the provisions of this Article shall be applied in determining whether any person has a permanent establishment in any State.

Article 4

Paragraph 2 of Article VII (Business Profits) of the Convention shall be deleted and replaced by the following:

> 2. Subject to the provisions of paragraph 3, where a resident of a Contracting State carries on, or has carried on, business in the other Contracting State through a permanent establishment situated therein, there shall in each Contracting State be attributed to that permanent establishment the business profits which it might be expected to make if it were a distinct and separate person engaged in the same or similar activities under the same or similar conditions and dealing wholly independently with the resident and with any other person related to the resident (within the meaning of paragraph 2 of Article IX (Related Persons)).

Article 5

1. Subparagraph 2(a) of Article X (Dividends) of the Convention shall be deleted and replaced by the following:

> (a) 5 percent of the gross amount of the dividends if the beneficial owner is a company which owns at least 10 percent of the voting stock of the company paying the dividends (for this purpose, a company that is a resident of a Contracting State shall be considered to own the voting stock owned by an entity that is considered fiscally transparent under the laws of that State and that is not a resident of the Contracting State of which the company paying the dividends is a resident, in proportion to the company's ownership interest in that entity);

2. Paragraph 3 of Article X (Dividends) of the Convention shall be deleted and replaced by the following:

3.   For the purposes of this Article, the term "dividends" means income from shares or other rights, not being debt-claims, participating in profits, as well as income that is subjected to the same taxation treatment as income from shares under the laws of the State of which the payer is a resident.

3.   Paragraph 4 of Article X (Dividends) of the Convention shall be deleted and replaced by the following:

4.   The provisions of paragraph 2 shall not apply if the beneficial owner of the dividends, being a resident of a Contracting State, carries on, or has carried on, business in the other Contracting State of which the company paying the dividends is a resident, through a permanent establishment situated therein, and the holding in respect of which the dividends are paid is effectively connected to such permanent establishment. In such case, the provisions of Article VII (Business Profits) shall apply.

4.   Paragraph 5 of Article X (Dividends) of the Convention shall be amended by deleting the words "or a fixed base" following the words "effectively connected with a permanent establishment".

5.   Subparagraph 7(c) of Article X (Dividends) of the Convention shall be deleted and replaced by the following:

(c)   Subparagraph 2(a) shall not apply to dividends paid by a resident of the United States that is a Real Estate Investment Trust (REIT), and subparagraph 2(b) shall apply only if:

(i)   The beneficial owner of the dividends is an individual holding an interest of not more than 10 percent in the REIT;

(ii)   The dividends are paid with respect to a class of stock that is publicly traded and the beneficial owner of the dividends is a person holding an interest of not more than 5 percent in any class of the REIT's stock; or

(iii)   The beneficial owner of the dividends is a person holding an interest of not more than 10 percent in the REIT and the REIT is diversified.

Otherwise, the rate of tax applicable under the domestic law of the United States shall apply. Where an estate or testamentary trust acquired its interest in a REIT as a consequence of an individual's death, for purposes of this subparagraph the estate or trust shall for the five-year period following the death be deemed with respect to that interest to be an individual.

Article 6

Article XI (Interest) of the Convention shall be deleted and replaced by the following:

Article XI

Interest

1.   Interest arising in a Contracting State and beneficially owned by a resident of the other Contracting State may be taxed only in that other State.

2.   The term "interest" as used in this Article means income from debt-claims of every kind, whether or not secured by mortgage, and whether or not carrying a right to participate in the debtor's profits, and in particular, income from government securities and income from bonds or debentures, including premiums or prizes attaching to such securities, bonds or debentures, as well as income assimilated to income from money lent by the taxation laws of the Contracting State in which the income arises. However, the term "interest" does not include income dealt with in Article X (Dividends).

3.   The provisions of paragraph 1 shall not apply if the beneficial owner of the interest, being a resident of a Contracting State, carries on, or has carried on, business in the other Contracting State in which the interest arises, through a permanent establishment situated therein, and the debt-claim in respect of which

the interest is paid is effectively connected with such permanent establishment. In such case the provisions of Article VII (Business Profits) shall apply.

4.   For the purposes of this Article, interest shall be deemed to arise in a Contracting State when the payer is that State itself, or a political subdivision, local authority or a resident of that State. Where, however, the person paying the interest, whether he is a resident of a Contracting State or not, has in a State other than that of which he is a resident a permanent establishment in connection with which the indebtedness on which the interest is paid was incurred, and such interest is borne by such permanent establishment, then such interest shall be deemed to arise in the State in which the permanent establishment is situated and not in the State of which the payer is a resident.

5.   Where, by reason of a special relationship between the payer and the beneficial owner or between both of them and some other person, the amount of the interest, having regard to the debt-claim for which it is paid, exceeds the amount which would have been agreed upon by the payer and the beneficial owner in the absence of such relationship, the provisions of this Article shall apply only to the last-mentioned amount. In such case the excess part of the payments shall remain taxable according to the laws of each Contracting State, due regard being had to the other provisions of this Convention.

6.   Notwithstanding the provisions of paragraph 1:

(a)   Interest arising in the United States that is contingent interest of a type that does not qualify as portfolio interest under United States law may be taxed by the United States but, if the beneficial owner of the interest is a resident of Canada, the gross amount of the interest may be taxed at a rate not exceeding the rate prescribed in subparagraph (b) of paragraph 2 of Article X (Dividends);

(b)   Interest arising in Canada that is determined with reference to receipts, sales, income, profits or other cash flow of the debtor or a related person, to any change in the value of any property of the debtor or a related person or to any dividend, partnership distribution or similar payment made by the debtor to a related person may be taxed by Canada, and according to the laws of Canada, but if the beneficial owner is a resident of the United States, the gross amount of the interest may be taxed at a rate not exceeding the rate prescribed in subparagraph (b) of paragraph 2 of Article X (Dividends); and

(c)   Interest that is an excess inclusion with respect to a residual interest in a real estate mortgage investment conduit may be taxed by each State in accordance with its domestic law.

7.   Where a resident of a Contracting State pays interest to a person other than a resident of the other Contracting State, that other State may not impose any tax on such interest except insofar as it arises in that other State or insofar as the debt-claim in respect of which the interest is paid is effectively connected with a permanent establishment situated in that other State.

Article 7

1.   Paragraph 5 of Article XII (Royalties) of the Convention shall be deleted and replaced by the following:

5.   The provisions of paragraphs 2 and 3 shall not apply if the beneficial owner of the royalties, being a resident of a Contracting State, carries on, or has carried on, business in the other Contracting State in which the royalties arise, through a permanent establishment situated therein, and the right or property in respect of which the royalties are paid is effectively connected to such permanent establishment. In such case the provisions of Article VII (Business Profits) shall apply.

2.   Subparagraph 6(a) of Article XII (Royalties) of the Convention shall be deleted and replaced by the following:

(a)   Royalties shall be deemed to arise in a Contracting State when the payer is a resident of that State. Where, however, the person paying the royalties, whether he is a resident of a Contracting State or not, has in a State a permanent establishment in connection with which the obligation to pay the royalties was incurred, and such royalties are borne by such permanent establishment, then such royalties shall be deemed to arise in the State in which the permanent establishment is situated and not in any other State of which the payer is a resident; and

3.   Paragraph 8 of Article XII (Royalties) of the Convention shall be amended by deleting the words "or a fixed base" following the words "effectively connected with a permanent establishment".

Article 8

1.   Paragraph 2 of Article XIII (Gains) of the Convention shall be deleted and replaced by the following:

2.   Gains from the alienation of personal property forming part of the business property of a permanent establishment which a resident of a Contracting State has or had (within the twelve-month period preceding the date of alienation) in the other Contracting State, including such gains from the alienation of such a permanent establishment, may be taxed in that other State.

2.   Paragraph 5 of Article XIII (Gains) of the Convention shall be deleted and replaced by the following:

5.   The provisions of paragraph 4 shall not affect the right of a Contracting State to levy, according to its domestic law, a tax on gains from the alienation of any property derived by an individual who is a resident of the other Contracting State if:

(a) The individual was a resident of the first-mentioned State:

    (i) For at least 120 months during any period of 20 consecutive years preceding the alienation of the property; and

    (ii) At any time during the 10 years immediately preceding the alienation of the property; and

(b) The property (or property for which such property was substituted in an alienation the gain on which was not recognized for the purposes of taxation in the first-mentioned State):

    (i) Was owned by the individual at the time the individual ceased to be a resident of the first-mentioned State; and

    (ii) Was not a property that the individual was treated as having alienated by reason of ceasing to be a resident of the first-mentioned State and becoming a resident of the other Contracting State.

3.   Paragraph 7 of Article XIII (Gains) of the Convention shall be deleted and replaced by the following:

7.   Where at any time an individual is treated for the purposes of taxation by a Contracting State as having alienated a property and is taxed in that State by reason thereof, the individual may elect to be treated for the purposes of taxation in the other Contracting State, in the year that includes that time and all subsequent years, as if the individual had, immediately before that time, sold and repurchased the property for an amount equal to its fair market value at that time.

4.   Subparagraph 9(c) of Article XIII (Gains) of the Convention shall be amended by deleting the words "or pertained to a fixed base" following the words "permanent establishment".

Article 9

Article XIV (Independent Personal Services) of the Convention shall be deleted and the succeeding Articles shall not be renumbered.

Article 10

1. The title of Article XV (Dependent Personal Services) of the Convention shall be deleted and replaced by "Income from Employment".

2. Paragraphs 1 and 2 of renamed Article XV (Income from Employment) of the Convention shall be deleted and replaced by the following:

    1. Subject to the provisions of Articles XVIII (Pensions and Annuities) and XIX (Government Service), salaries, wages and other remuneration derived by a resident of a Contracting State in respect of an employment shall be taxable only in that State unless the employment is exercised in the other Contracting State. If the employment is so exercised, such remuneration as is derived therefrom may be taxed in that other State.

    2. Notwithstanding the provisions of paragraph 1, remuneration derived by a resident of a Contracting State in respect of an employment exercised in the other Contracting State shall be taxable only in the first-mentioned State if:

        (a) Such remuneration does not exceed ten thousand dollars ($10,000) in the currency of that other State; or

        (b) The recipient is present in that other State for a period or periods not exceeding in the aggregate 183 days in any twelve-month period commencing or ending in the fiscal year concerned, and the remuneration is not paid by, or on behalf of, a person who is a resident of that other State and is not borne by a permanent establishment in that other State.

Article 11

1.   Paragraph 1 of Article XVI (Artistes and Athletes) shall be amended by deleting the words "XIV (Independent Personal Services)" following the words "Notwithstanding the provisions of Articles" and replacing them with the words "VII (Business Profits)" and by deleting the words "XV (Dependent Personal Services)" and replacing them with the words "XV (Income from Employment)".

2.   Paragraph 2 of Article XVI (Artistes and Athletes) shall be amended by deleting the words "XIV (Independent Personal Services)" following the words "notwithstanding the provisions of Articles VII (Business Profits)," and by deleting the words "XV (Dependent Personal Services)" and replacing them with the words "XV (Income from Employment)".

3.   Paragraph 4 of Article XVI (Artistes and Athletes) shall be amended by deleting the words "XIV (Independent Personal Services)" following the words "Notwithstanding the provisions of Articles" and replacing them with the words "VII (Business Profits)" and by deleting the words "(Dependent Personal Services)" in both places they appear in the paragraph and replacing them with the words "(Income from Employment)".

Article 12

Article XVII (Withholding of Taxes in Respect of Personal Services) of the Convention shall be deleted and the succeeding Articles shall not be renumbered.

Article 13

1.   Paragraphs 3 and 4 of Article XVIII (Pensions and Annuities) of the Convention shall be deleted and replaced by the following:

      3.   For the purposes of this Convention:

(a)   The term "pensions" includes any payment under a superannuation, pension or other retirement arrangement, Armed Forces retirement pay, war veterans pensions and allowances and amounts paid under a sickness, accident or disability plan, but does not include payments under an income-averaging annuity contract or, except for the purposes of Article XIX (Government Service), any benefit referred to in paragraph 5; and

(b)   The term "pensions" also includes a Roth IRA, within the meaning of section 408A of the Internal Revenue Code, or a plan or arrangement created pursuant to legislation enacted by a Contracting State after September 21, 2007 that the competent authorities have agreed is similar thereto. Notwithstanding the provisions of the preceding sentence, from such time that contributions have been made to the Roth IRA or similar plan or arrangement, by or for the benefit of a resident of the other Contracting State (other than rollover contributions from a Roth IRA or similar plan or arrangement described in the previous sentence that is a pension within the meaning of this subparagraph), to the extent of accretions from such time, such Roth IRA or similar plan or arrangement shall cease to be considered a pension for purposes of the provisions of this Article.

4.   For the purposes of this Convention:

(a)   The term "annuity" means a stated sum paid periodically at stated times during life or during a specified number of years, under an obligation to make the payments in return for adequate and full consideration (other than services rendered), but does not include a payment that is not a periodic payment or any annuity the cost of which was deductible for the purposes of taxation in the Contracting State in which it was acquired; and

(b)   An annuity or other amount paid in respect of a life insurance or
annuity contract (including a withdrawal in respect of the cash value
thereof) shall be deemed to arise in a Contracting State if the person
paying the annuity or other amount (in this subparagraph referred to as
the "payer") is a resident of that State. However, if the payer, whether a
resident of a Contracting State or not, has in a State other than that of
which the payer is a resident a permanent establishment in connection
with which the obligation giving rise to the annuity or other amount was
incurred, and the annuity or other amount is borne by the permanent
establishment, then the annuity or other amount shall be deemed to arise
in the State in which the permanent establishment is situated and not in
the State of which the payer is a resident.

2.   Paragraph 7 of Article XVIII (Pensions and Annuities) of the Convention shall be
deleted and replaced by the following:

7.   A natural person who is a citizen or resident of a Contracting State and a
beneficiary of a trust, company, organization or other arrangement that is a
resident of the other Contracting State, generally exempt from income taxation
in that other State and operated exclusively to provide pension or employee
benefits may elect to defer taxation in the first-mentioned State, subject to rules
established by the competent authority of that State, with respect to any income
accrued in the plan but not distributed by the plan, until such time as and to the
extent that a distribution is made from the plan or any plan substituted therefor.

3.   Article XVIII (Pensions and Annuities) of the Convention shall be amended by adding
the following paragraphs:

8.   Contributions made to, or benefits accrued under, a qualifying retirement
plan in a Contracting State by or on behalf of an individual shall be deductible
or excludible in computing the individual's taxable income in the other
Contracting State, and contributions made to the plan by the individual's

employer shall be allowed as a deduction in computing the employer's profits in that other State, where:

(a)   The individual performs services as an employee in that other State the remuneration from which is taxable in that other State;

(b)   The individual was participating in the plan (or another similar plan for which this plan was substituted) immediately before the individual began performing the services in that other State;

(c)   The individual was not a resident of that other State immediately before the individual began performing the services in that other State;

(d)   The individual has performed services in that other State for the same employer (or a related employer) for no more than 60 of the 120 months preceding the individual's current taxation year;

(e)   The contributions and benefits are attributable to the services performed by the individual in that other State, and are made or accrued during the period in which the individual performs those services; and

(f)   With respect to contributions and benefits that are attributable to services performed during a period in the individual's current taxation year, no contributions in respect of the period are made by or on behalf of the individual to, and no services performed in that other State during the period are otherwise taken into account for purposes of determining the individual's entitlement to benefits under, any plan that would be a qualifying retirement plan in that other State if paragraph 15 of this Article were read without reference to subparagraphs (b) and (c) of that paragraph.

This paragraph shall apply only to the extent that the contributions or benefits would qualify for tax relief in the first-mentioned State if the individual was a resident of and performed the services in that State.

9.   For the purposes of United States taxation, the benefits granted under paragraph 8 to a citizen of the United States shall not exceed the benefits that would be allowed by the United States to its residents for contributions to, or benefits otherwise accrued under, a generally corresponding pension or retirement plan established in and recognized for tax purposes by the United States.

10.   Contributions made to, or benefits accrued under, a qualifying retirement plan in a Contracting State by or on behalf of an individual who is a resident of the other Contracting State shall be deductible or excludible in computing the individual's taxable income in that other State, where:

(a)   The individual performs services as an employee in the first-mentioned state the remuneration from which is taxable in that State and is borne by an employer who is a resident of that State or by a permanent establishment which the employer has in that State; and

(b)   The contributions and benefits are attributable to those services and are made or accrued during the period in which the individual performs those services.

This paragraph shall apply only to the extent that the contributions or benefits qualify for tax relief in the first-mentioned State.

11.   For the purposes of Canadian taxation, the amount of contributions otherwise allowed as a deduction under paragraph 10 to an individual for a taxation year shall not exceed the individual's deduction limit under the law of Canada for the year for contributions to registered retirement savings plans remaining after taking into account the amount of contributions to registered retirement savings plans deducted by the individual under the law of Canada for the year. The amount deducted by an individual under paragraph 10 for a taxation year shall be taken into account in computing the individual's deduction

limit under the law of Canada for subsequent taxation years for contributions to registered retirement savings plans.

12.   For the purposes of United States taxation, the benefits granted under paragraph 10 shall not exceed the benefits that would be allowed by the United States to its residents for contributions to, or benefits otherwise accrued under, a generally corresponding pension or retirement plan established in and recognized for tax purposes by the United States. For purposes of determining an individual's eligibility to participate in and receive tax benefits with respect to a pension or retirement plan or other retirement arrangement established in and recognized for tax purposes by the United States, contributions made to, or benefits accrued under, a qualifying retirement plan in Canada by or on behalf of the individual shall be treated as contributions or benefits under a generally corresponding pension or retirement plan established in and recognized for tax purposes by the United States.

13.   Contributions made to, or benefits accrued under, a qualifying retirement plan in Canada by or on behalf of a citizen of the United States who is a resident of Canada shall be deductible or excludible in computing the citizen's taxable income in the United States, where:

    (a)   The citizen performs services as an employee in Canada the remuneration from which is taxable in Canada and is borne by an employer who is a resident of Canada or by a permanent establishment which the employer has in Canada; and

    (b)   The contributions and benefits are attributable to those services and are made or accrued during the period in which the citizen performs those services.

This paragraph shall apply only to the extent that the contributions or benefits qualify for tax relief in Canada.

14.   The benefits granted under paragraph 13 shall not exceed the benefits that would be allowed by the United States to its residents for contributions to,

or benefits otherwise accrued under, a generally corresponding pension or retirement plan established in and recognized for tax purposes by the United States. For purposes of determining an individual's eligibility to participate in and receive tax benefits with respect to a pension or retirement plan or other retirement arrangement established in and recognized for tax purposes by the United States, contributions made to, or benefits accrued under, a qualifying retirement plan in Canada by or on behalf of the individual shall be treated as contributions or benefits under a generally corresponding pension or retirement plan established in and recognized for tax purposes by the United States.

15.   For purposes of paragraphs 8 to 14, a qualifying retirement plan in a Contracting State means a trust, company, organization or other arrangement:

   (a)   That is a resident of that State, generally exempt from income taxation in that State and operated primarily to provide pension or retirement benefits;

   (b)   That is not an individual arrangement in respect of which the individual's employer has no involvement; and

   (c)   Which the competent authority of the other Contracting State agrees generally corresponds to a pension or retirement plan established in and recognized for tax purposes by that other State.

16.   For purposes of this Article, a distribution from a pension or retirement plan that is reasonably attributable to a contribution or benefit for which a benefit was allowed pursuant to paragraph 8, 10 or 13 shall be deemed to arise in the Contracting State in which the plan is established.

17.   Paragraphs 8 to 16 apply, with such modifications as the circumstances require, as though the relationship between a partnership that carries on a business, and an individual who is a member of the partnership, were that of employer and employee.

Article 14

Article XIX (Government Service) of the Convention shall be amended by deleting the words "XIV (Independent Personal Services)" and replacing them with the words "VII (Business Profits)" and by deleting the words "XV (Dependent Personal Services)" and replacing them with the words "XV (Income from Employment)".

Article 15

Article XX (Students) of the Convention shall be deleted and replaced by the following:

Payments received by an individual who is a student, apprentice, or business trainee, and is, or was immediately before visiting a Contracting State, a resident of the other Contracting State, and who is present in the first-mentioned State for the purpose of the individual's full-time education or full-time training, shall not be taxed in that State, provided that such payments arise outside that State, and are for the purpose of the maintenance, education or training of the individual. The provisions of this Article shall apply to an apprentice or business trainee only for a period of time not exceeding one year from the date the individual first arrives in the first-mentioned State for the purpose of the individual's training.

Article 16

1.   Paragraphs 4, 5 and 6 of Article XXI (Exempt Organizations) of the Convention shall be renumbered as paragraphs 5, 6 and 7 respectively.

2.   Paragraphs 1 through 3 of Article XXI (Exempt Organizations) of the Convention shall be deleted and replaced by the following four paragraphs:

1.   Subject to the provisions of paragraph 4, income derived by a religious, scientific, literary, educational or charitable organization shall be exempt from

tax in a Contracting State if it is resident in the other Contracting State, but only to the extent that such income is exempt from tax in that other State.

2.   Subject to the provisions of paragraph 4, income referred to in Articles X (Dividends) and XI (Interest) derived by a trust, company, organization or other arrangement that is a resident of a Contracting State, generally exempt from income taxation in a taxable year in that State and operated exclusively to administer or provide pension, retirement or employee benefits shall be exempt from income taxation in that taxable year in the other Contracting State.

3.   Subject to the provisions of paragraph 4, income referred to in Articles X (Dividends) and XI (Interest) derived by a trust, company, organization or other arrangement that is a resident of a Contracting State, generally exempt from income taxation in a taxable year in that State and operated exclusively to earn income for the benefit of one or more of the following:

    (a)   An organization referred to in paragraph 1; or

    (b)   A trust, company, organization or other arrangement
    referred to in paragraph 2;

shall be exempt from income taxation in that taxable year in the other Contracting State.

4.   The provisions of paragraphs 1, 2 and 3 shall not apply with respect to the income of a trust, company, organization or other arrangement from carrying on a trade or business or from a related person other than a person referred to in paragraphs 1, 2 or 3.

Article 17

Article XXII (Other Income) of the Convention shall be amended by adding the following paragraph:

4.   Notwithstanding the provisions of paragraph 1, compensation derived by a resident of a Contracting State in respect of the provision of a guarantee of indebtedness shall be taxable only in that State, unless such compensation is business profits attributable to a permanent establishment situated in the other Contracting State, in which case the provisions of Article VII (Business Profits) shall apply.

Article 18

Paragraph 2 of Article XXIII (Capital) of the Convention shall be amended by deleting the phrase ", or by personal property pertaining to a fixed base available to a resident of a Contracting State in the other Contracting State for the purpose of performing independent personal services,".

Article 19

Subparagraph 2(b) of Article XXIV (Elimination of Double Taxation) of the Convention shall be deleted and replaced with the following:

(b)   In the case of a company which is a resident of Canada owning at least 10 percent of the voting stock of a company which is a resident of the United States from which it receives dividends in any taxable year, Canada shall allow as a credit against the Canadian tax on income the appropriate amount of income tax paid or accrued to the United States by the second company with respect to the profits out of which the dividends are paid.

Article 20

1.   Paragraph 1 of Article XXV (Non-Discrimination) of the Convention shall be deleted and replaced by the following:

>   1.   Nationals of a Contracting State shall not be subjected in the other Contracting State to any taxation or any requirement connected therewith that is more burdensome than the taxation and connected requirements to which nationals of that other State in the same circumstances, particularly with respect to taxation on worldwide income, are or may be subjected. This provision shall also apply to individuals who are not residents of one or both of the Contracting States.

2.   Paragraph 2 of Article XXV (Non-Discrimination) of the Convention shall be deleted, and paragraphs 3 to 10 of Article XXV shall be renumbered accordingly.

3.   Renumbered paragraph 3 of Article XXV (Non-Discrimination) of the Convention shall be amended by deleting the words "Article XV (Dependent Personal Services)" and replacing them with the words "Article XV (Income from Employment)".

Article 21

1.   Paragraph 6 of Article XXVI (Mutual Agreement Procedure) of the Convention shall be deleted and replaced by the following:

>   6.   Where, pursuant to a mutual agreement procedure under this Article, the competent authorities have endeavored but are unable to reach a complete agreement in a case, the case shall be resolved through arbitration conducted in the manner prescribed by, and subject to, the requirements of paragraph 7 and any rules or procedures agreed upon by the Contracting States by notes to be exchanged through diplomatic channels, if:

(a)   Tax returns have been filed with at least one of the Contracting States with respect to the taxable years at issue in the case;

(b)   The case:

    (i)   Is a case that:

        (A)   Involves the application of one or more Articles that the competent authorities have agreed in an exchange of notes shall be the subject of arbitration; and

        (B)   Is not a particular case that the competent authorities agree, before the date on which arbitration proceedings would otherwise have begun, is not suitable for determination by arbitration; or

    (ii)   Is a particular case that the competent authorities agree is suitable for determination by arbitration; and

(c)   All concerned persons agree according to the provisions of subparagraph 7(d).

7.   For the purposes of paragraph 6 and this paragraph, the following rules and definitions shall apply:

(a)   The term "concerned person" means the presenter of a case to a competent authority for consideration under this Article and all other persons, if any, whose tax liability to either Contracting State may be directly affected by a mutual agreement arising from that consideration;

(b)   The "commencement date" for a case is the earliest date on which the information necessary to undertake substantive consideration for a mutual agreement has been received by both competent authorities;

(c)   Arbitration proceedings in a case shall begin on the later of:

    (i)   Two years after the commencement date of that case, unless both competent authorities have previously agreed to a different date, and

(ii)   The earliest date upon which the agreement required by subparagraph (d) has been received by both competent authorities;

(d)   The concerned person(s), and their authorized representatives or agents, must agree prior to the beginning of arbitration proceedings not to disclose to any other person any information received during the course of the arbitration proceeding from either Contracting State or the arbitration board, other than the determination of such board;

(e)   Unless a concerned person does not accept the determination of an arbitration board, the determination shall constitute a resolution by mutual agreement under this Article and shall be binding on both Contracting States with respect to that case; and

(f)   For purposes of an arbitration proceeding under paragraph 6 and this paragraph, the members of the arbitration board and their staffs shall be considered "persons or authorities" to whom information may be disclosed under Article XXVII (Exchange of Information) of this Convention.

Article 22

1.   Subparagraph 8(a) of Article XXVI A (Assistance in Collection) of the Convention shall be deleted and replaced by the following:

(a)   Where the taxpayer is an individual, the revenue claim relates either to a taxable period in which the taxpayer was a citizen of the requested State or, if the taxpayer became a citizen of the requested State at any time before November 9, 1995 and is such a citizen at the time the applicant State applies for collection of the claim, to a taxable period that ended before November 9, 1995; and

2.   Paragraph 9 of Article XXVI A (Assistance in Collection) of the Convention shall be deleted and replaced by the following:

>   9.   Notwithstanding the provisions of Article II (Taxes Covered), the provisions of this Article shall apply to all categories of taxes collected, and to contributions to social security and employment insurance premiums levied, by or on behalf of the Government of a Contracting State.

Article 23

Article XXVII (Exchange of Information) of the Convention shall be deleted and replaced by the following:

Article XXVII

Exchange of Information

1.   The competent authorities of the Contracting States shall exchange such information as may be relevant for carrying out the provisions of this Convention or of the domestic laws of the Contracting States concerning taxes to which this Convention applies insofar as the taxation thereunder is not contrary to this Convention. The exchange of information is not restricted by Article I (Personal Scope). Any information received by a Contracting State shall be treated as secret in the same manner as information obtained under the taxation laws of that State and shall be disclosed only to persons or authorities (including courts and administrative bodies) involved in the assessment or collection of, the administration and enforcement in respect of, or the determination of appeals in relation to the taxes to which this Convention applies or, notwithstanding paragraph 4, in relation to taxes imposed by a political subdivision or local authority of a Contracting State that are substantially similar to the taxes covered by this Convention under Article II (Taxes Covered). Such persons or authorities shall use the information only for

such purposes. They may disclose the information in public court proceedings or in judicial decisions. The competent authorities may release to an arbitration board established pursuant to paragraph 6 of Article XXVI (Mutual Agreement Procedure) such information as is necessary for carrying out the arbitration procedure; the members of the arbitration board shall be subject to the limitations on disclosure described in this Article.

2.   If information is requested by a Contracting State in accordance with this Article, the other Contracting State shall use its information gathering measures to obtain the requested information, even though that other State may not need such information for its own tax purposes. The obligation contained in the preceding sentence is subject to the limitations of paragraph 3 but in no case shall such limitations be construed to permit a Contracting State to decline to supply information because it has no domestic interest in such information.

3.   In no case shall the provisions of paragraph 1 and 2 be construed so as to impose on a Contracting State the obligation:

(a)   To carry out administrative measures at variance with the laws and administrative practice of that State or of the other Contracting State;

(b)   To supply information which is not obtainable under the laws or in the normal course of the administration of that State or of the other Contracting State; or

(c)   To supply information which would disclose any trade, business, industrial, commercial or professional secret or trade process, or information the disclosure of which would be contrary to public policy (ordre public).

4.   For the purposes of this Article, this Convention shall apply, notwithstanding the provisions of Article II (Taxes Covered):

(a)   To all taxes imposed by a Contracting State; and

(b)   To other taxes to which any other provision of this Convention applies, but only to the extent that the information may be relevant for the purposes of the application of that provision.

5.   In no case shall the provisions of paragraph 3 be construed to permit a Contracting State to decline to supply information because the information is held by a bank, other financial institution, nominee or person acting in an agency or a fiduciary capacity or because it relates to ownership interests in a person.

6.   If specifically requested by the competent authority of a Contracting State, the competent authority of the other Contracting State shall provide information under this Article in the form of depositions of witnesses and authenticated copies of unedited original documents (including books, papers, statements, records, accounts, and writings).

7.   The requested State shall allow representatives of the requesting State to enter the requested State to interview individuals and examine books and records with the consent of the persons subject to examination.

Article 24

1.   Paragraph 2 of Article XXIX (Miscellaneous Rules) of the Convention shall be deleted and replaced by the following:

2.   (a)   Except to the extent provided in paragraph 3, this Convention shall not affect the taxation by a Contracting State of its residents (as determined under Article IV (Residence)) and, in the case of the United States, its citizens and companies electing to be treated as domestic corporations.

(b)   Notwithstanding the other provisions of this Convention, a former citizen or former long-term resident of the United States, may, for the period of ten years following the loss of such status, be taxed in accordance with the laws of the United States with respect to income from sources within the United States (including income deemed under the domestic law of the United States to arise from such sources).

2.   Subparagraph 3(a) of Article XXIX (Miscellaneous Rules) shall be deleted and replaced by the following:

>   (a)   Under paragraphs 3 and 4 of Article IX (Related Persons), paragraphs 6 and 7 of Article XIII (Gains), paragraphs 1, 3, 4, 5, 6(b), 7, 8, 10 and 13 of Article XVIII (Pensions and Annuities), paragraph 5 of Article XXIX (Miscellaneous Rules), paragraphs 1, 5, and 6 of Article XXIX B (Taxes Imposed by Reason of Death), paragraphs 2, 3, 4, and 7 of Article XXIX B (Taxes Imposed by Reason of Death) as applied to estates of persons other than former citizens referred to in paragraph 2 of this Article, paragraphs 3 and 5 of Article XXX (Entry into Force), and Articles XIX (Government Service), XXI (Exempt Organizations), XXIV (Elimination of Double Taxation), XXV (Non-Discrimination) and XXVI (Mutual Agreement Procedure);

Article 25

Article XXIX A (Limitation on Benefits) of the Convention shall be deleted and replaced by the following:

Article XXIX A

Limitation on Benefits

1.   For the purposes of the application of this Convention by a Contracting State,

>   (a)   a qualifying person shall be entitled to all of the benefits of this Convention; and

(b)   except as provided in paragraphs 3, 4 and 6, a person that is not a qualifying person shall not be entitled to any benefits of this Convention.

2.   For the purposes of this Article, a qualifying person is a resident of a Contracting State that is:

(a)   a natural person;

(b)   a Contracting State or a political subdivision or local authority thereof, or any agency or instrumentality of any such State, subdivision or authority;

(c)   a company or trust whose principal class of shares or units (and any disproportionate class of shares or units) is primarily and regularly traded on one or more recognized stock exchanges;

(d)   a company, if five or fewer persons each of which is a company or trust referred to in subparagraph (c) own directly or indirectly more than 50 percent of the aggregate vote and value of the shares and more than 50 percent of the vote and value of each disproportionate class of shares (in neither case including debt substitute shares), provided that each company or trust in the chain of ownership is a qualifying person;

(e)   (i)   a company, 50 percent or more of the aggregate vote and value of the shares of which and 50 percent or more of the vote and value of each disproportionate class of shares (in neither case including debt substitute shares) of which is not owned, directly or indirectly, by persons other than qualifying persons; or

(ii)   a trust, 50 percent or more of the beneficial interest in which and 50 percent or more of each disproportionate interest in which, is not owned, directly or indirectly, by persons other than qualifying persons;

where the amount of the expenses deductible from gross income (as determined in the State of residence of the company or trust) that are paid or payable by the company or trust, as the case may be, for its preceding fiscal period (or, in the case of its first fiscal period, that period) directly or indirectly, to persons that are not qualifying persons is less than 50 percent of its gross income for that period;

(f)   an estate;

(g)   a not-for-profit organization, provided that more than half of the beneficiaries, members or participants of the organization are qualifying persons;

(h)   a trust, company, organization or other arrangement described in paragraph 2 of Article XXI (Exempt Organizations) and established for the purpose of providing benefits primarily to individuals who are qualifying persons, or persons who were qualifying persons within the five preceding years; or

(i)   a trust, company, organization or other arrangement described in paragraph 3 of Article XXI (Exempt Organizations) provided that the beneficiaries of the trust, company, organization or other arrangement are described in subparagraph (g) or (h).

3.   Where a person is a resident of a Contracting State and is not a qualifying person, and that person, or a person related thereto, is engaged in the active conduct of a trade or business in that State (other than the business of making or managing investments, unless those activities are carried on with customers in the ordinary course of business by a bank, an insurance company, a registered securities dealer or a deposit-taking financial institution), the benefits of this Convention shall apply to that resident person with respect to income derived from the other Contracting State in connection with or incidental to that trade or business (including any such income derived directly or indirectly by that resident person through one or more other persons that are residents of that

other State), but only if that trade or business is substantial in relation to the activity carried on in that other State giving rise to the income in respect of which benefits provided under this Convention by that other State are claimed.

4.   A company that is a resident of a Contracting State shall also be entitled to the benefits of Articles X (Dividends), XI (Interest) and XII (Royalties) if:

(a)   Its shares that represent more than 90 percent of the aggregate vote and value of all of its shares and at least 50 percent of the vote and value of any disproportionate class of shares (in neither case including debt substitute shares) are owned, directly or indirectly, by persons each of whom is a qualifying person or a person who:

(i)   Is a resident of a country with which the other Contracting State has a comprehensive income tax convention and is entitled to all of the benefits provided by that other State under that convention;

(ii)   Would qualify for benefits under paragraphs 2 or 3 if that person were a resident of the first-mentioned State (and, for the purposes of paragraph 3, if the business it carried on in the country of which it is a resident were carried on by it in the first-mentioned State); and

(iii)   Would be entitled to a rate of tax in the other Contracting State under the convention between that person's country of residence and that other State, in respect of the particular class of income for which benefits are being claimed under this Convention, that is at least as low as the rate applicable under this Convention; and

(b)   The amount of the expenses deductible from gross income (as determined in the company's State of residence) that are paid or payable by the company for its preceding fiscal period (or, in the case of its first fiscal period, that period) directly or indirectly to persons that are not qualifying persons is less than 50 percent of the company's gross income for that period.

5.   For the purposes of this Article,

   (a)   The term "debt substitute share" means:

      (i)   A share described in paragraph (e) of the definition "term preferred share" in the Income Tax Act, as it may be amended from time to time without changing the general principle thereof; and

      (ii)   Such other type of share as may be agreed upon by the competent authorities of the Contracting States.

   (b)   The term "disproportionate class of shares" means any class of shares of a company resident in one of the Contracting States that entitles the shareholder to disproportionately higher participation, through dividends, redemption payments or otherwise, in the earnings generated in the other State by particular assets or activities of the company;

   (c)   The term "disproportionate interest in a trust" means any interest in a trust resident in one of the Contracting States that entitles the interest holder to disproportionately higher participation in, or claim to, the earnings generated in the other State by particular assets or activities of the trust;

   (d)   The term "not-for-profit organization" of a Contracting State means an entity created or established in that State and that is, by reason of its not-for-profit status, generally exempt from income taxation in that State, and includes a private foundation, charity, trade union, trade association or similar organization;

   (e)   The term "principal class of shares" of a company means the ordinary or common shares of the company, provided that such class of shares represents the majority of the voting power and value of the company. If no single class of ordinary or common shares represents the majority of the aggregate voting power and value of the company, the "principal class of shares" are those classes that in the aggregate represent a majority of the aggregate voting power and value of the company; and

    (f)   The term "recognized stock exchange" means:

        (i)   The NASDAQ System owned by the National Association of Securities Dealers, Inc. and any stock exchange registered with the Securities and Exchange Commission as a national securities exchange for purposes of the Securities Exchange Act of 1934;

        (ii)   Canadian stock exchanges that are "prescribed stock exchanges" or "designated stock exchanges" under the Income Tax Act; and

        (iii)   Any other stock exchange agreed upon by the Contracting States in an exchange of notes or by the competent authorities of the Contracting States.

6.   Where a person that is a resident of a Contracting State is not entitled under the preceding provisions of this Article to the benefits provided under this Convention by the other Contracting State, the competent authority of that other State shall, upon that person's request, determine on the basis of all factors including the history, structure, ownership and operations of that person whether:

    (a)   Its creation and existence did not have as a principal purpose the obtaining of benefits under this Convention that would not otherwise be available; or

    (b)   It would not be appropriate, having regard to the purpose of this Article, to deny the benefits of this Convention to that person.

The person shall be granted the benefits of this Convention by that other State where the competent authority determines that subparagraph (a) or (b) applies.

7.   It is understood that this Article shall not be construed as restricting in any manner the right of a Contracting State to deny benefits under this Convention where it can reasonably be concluded that to do otherwise would result in an abuse of the provisions of this Convention.

Article 26

1.   Paragraph 1 of Article XXIX B (Taxes Imposed by Reason of Death) of the Convention shall be deleted and replaced by the following:

1.   Where the property of an individual who is a resident of a Contracting State passes by reason of the individual's death to an organization that is referred to in paragraph 1 of Article XXI (Exempt Organizations) and that is a resident of the other Contracting State,

(a)   If the individual is a resident of the United States and the organization is a resident of Canada, the tax consequences in the United States arising out of the passing of the property shall apply as if the organization were a resident of the United States; and

(b)   If the individual is a resident of Canada and the organization is a resident of the United States, the tax consequences in Canada arising out of the passing of the property shall apply as if the individual had disposed of the property for proceeds equal to an amount elected on behalf of the individual for this purpose (in a manner specified by the competent authority of Canada), which amount shall be no less than the individual's cost of the property as determined for purposes of Canadian tax and no greater than the fair market value of the property.

2.   Paragraph 5 of Article XXIX B (Taxes Imposed by Reason of Death) of the Convention shall be deleted and replaced by the following:

> 5.   Where an individual was a resident of the United States immediately before the individual's death, for the purposes of subsections 70(5.2) and (6) of the Income Tax Act, both the individual and the individual's spouse shall be deemed to have been resident in Canada immediately before the individual's death. Where a trust that would be a trust described in subsection 70(6) of that Act, if its trustees that were residents or citizens of the United States or domestic corporations under the law of the United States were residents of Canada, requests the competent authority of Canada to do so, the competent authority may agree, subject to terms and conditions satisfactory to such competent authority, to treat the trust for the purposes of that Act as being resident in Canada for such time and with respect to such property as may be stipulated in the agreement.

Article 27

1.   This Protocol shall be subject to ratification in accordance with the applicable procedures in the United States and Canada. The Contracting States shall notify each other in writing, through diplomatic channels, when their respective applicable procedures have been satisfied.

2.   This Protocol shall enter into force on the date of the later of the notifications referred to in paragraph 1, or January 1, 2008, whichever is later. The provisions of this Protocol shall have effect:

> (a)   In respect of taxes withheld at source, for amounts paid or credited on or after the first day of the second month that begins after the date on which this Protocol enters into force;

(b)   In respect of other taxes, for taxable years that begin after (or, if the later of the notifications referred to in paragraph 1 is dated in 2007, taxable years that begin in and after) the calendar year in which this Protocol enters into force.

3.   Notwithstanding paragraph 2,

(a)   Paragraph 1 of Article 2 of this Protocol shall have effect with respect to corporate continuations effected after September 17, 2000;

(b)   New paragraph 7 of Article IV (Residence) of the Convention as added by Article 2 of this Protocol shall have effect as of the first day of the third calendar year that ends after this Protocol enters into force;

(c)   Article 3 of this Protocol shall have effect as of the third taxable year that ends after this Protocol enters into force, but in no event shall it apply to include, in the determination of whether an enterprise is deemed to provide services through a permanent establishment under paragraph 9 of Article V (Permanent Establishment) of the Convention, any days of presence, services rendered, or gross active business revenues that occur or arise prior to January 1, 2010;

(d)   In applying Article 6 of this Protocol to interest paid or credited during the first two calendar years that end after entry into force of this Protocol, paragraph 1 of Article XI (Interest) of the Convention shall be read as follows:

1.   Interest arising in a Contracting State and beneficially owned by a resident of the other Contracting State may be taxed only in that other State. However, if the interest is not exempt under paragraph 3 of Article XI (Interest) as it read on January 1, 2007, and the payer of the interest and the beneficial owner of the interest are related, or would be deemed to be related if the provisions of paragraph 2 of Article IX (Related Persons) applied for this purpose, such interest may also be taxed in the Contracting State in which it arises, and according to the laws of that State, but the tax so charged shall not exceed the following percentage of the gross amount of the interest:

(a)   If the interest is paid or credited during the first calendar year that ends after entry into force of this paragraph, 7 percent; and

(b)   If the interest is paid or credited during the second calendar year that ends after entry into force of this paragraph, 4 percent;

(e)   Paragraphs 2 and 3 of Article 8 of this Protocol shall have effect with respect to alienations of property that occur (including, for greater certainty, those that are deemed under the law of a Contracting State to occur) after September 17, 2000;

(f)   Article 21 of this Protocol shall have effect with respect to

(i)   Cases that are under consideration by the competent authorities as of the date on which this Protocol enters into force; and

(ii)   Cases that come under such consideration after that time,

and the commencement date for a case described in subparagraph (f)(i) shall be the date on which the Protocol enters into force; and

(g)   Article 22 of this Protocol shall have effect for revenue claims finally determined by an applicant State after November 9, 1985.

IN WITNESS WHEREOF the undersigned, being duly authorized thereto by their respective Governments, have signed this Protocol.

DONE in duplicate at Chelsea this twenty-first day of September 2007 in the English and French languages, each text being equally authentic.

FOR THE GOVERNMENT OF
THE UNITED STATES OF AMERICA:

FOR THE GOVERNMENT OF
CANADA: